LAYERS OF LEARNING

YEAR THREE • UNIT FIVE

RENAISSANCE ENGLAND
TANZANIA & KENYA
MAMMALS
SHAKESPEARE

Published by HooDoo Publishing
United States of America
© 2014 Layers of Learning
Copies of maps or activities may be made for a particular family or classroom.
ISBN 978-1500959920

Units At A Glance: Topics For All Four Years of the Layers of Learning Program

1	History	Geography	Science	The Arts
1	Mesopotamia	Maps & Globes	Planets	Cave Paintings
2	Egypt	Map Keys	Stars	Egyptian Art
3	Europe	Global Grids	Earth & Moon	Crafts
4	Ancient Greece	Wonders	Satellites	Greek Art
5	Babylon	Mapping People	Humans in Space	Poetry
6	The Levant	Physical Earth	Laws of Motion	List Poems
7	Phoenicians	Oceans	Motion	Moral Stories
8	Assyrians	Deserts	Fluids	Rhythm
9	Persians	Arctic	Waves	Melody
10	Ancient China	Forests	Machines	Chinese Art
11	Early Japan	Mountains	States of Matter	Line & Shape
12	Arabia	Rivers & Lakes	Atoms	Color & Value
13	Ancient India	Grasslands	Elements	Texture & Form
14	Ancient Africa	Africa	Bonding	African Tales
15	First North Americans	North America	Salts	Creative Kids
16	Ancient South America	South America	Plants	South American Art
17	Celts	Europe	Flowering Plants	Jewelry
18	Roman Republic	Asia	Trees	Roman Art
19	Christianity	Australia & Oceania	Simple Plants	Instruments
20	Roman Empire	You Explore	Fungi	Composing Music

2	History	Geography	Science	The Arts
1	Byzantines	Turkey	Climate & Seasons	Byzantine Art
2	Barbarians	Ireland	Forecasting	Illumination
3	Islam	Arabian Peninsula	Clouds & Precipitation	Creative Kids
4	Vikings	Norway	Special Effects	Viking Art
5	Anglo Saxons	Britain	Wild Weather	King Arthur Tales
6	Charlemagne	France	Cells and DNA	Carolingian Art
7	Normans	Nigeria	Skeletons	Canterbury Tales
8	Feudal System	Germany	Muscles, Skin, & Cardiopulmonary	Gothic Art
9	Crusades	Balkans	Digestive & Senses	Religious Art
10	Burgundy, Venice, Spain	Switzerland	Nerves	Oil Paints
11	Wars of the Roses	Russia	Health	Minstrels & Plays
12	Eastern Europe	Hungary	Metals	Printmaking
13	African Kingdoms	Mali	Carbon Chem	Textiles
14	Asian Kingdoms	Southeast Asia	Non-metals	Vivid Language
15	Mongols	Caucasus	Gases	Fun With Poetry
16	Medieval China & Japan	China	Electricity	Asian Arts
17	Pacific Peoples	Micronesia	Circuits	Arts of the Islands
18	American Peoples	Canada	Technology	Indian Legends
19	The Renaissance	Italy	Magnetism	Renaissance Art I
20	Explorers	Caribbean Sea	Motors	Renaissance Art II

3	History	Geography	Science	The Arts
1	Age of Exploration	Argentina and Chile	Classification & Insects	Fairy Tales
2	The Ottoman Empire	Egypt and Libya	Reptiles & Amphibians	Poetry
3	Mogul Empire	Pakistan & Afghanistan	Fish	Mogul Arts
4	Reformation	Angola & Zambia	Birds	Reformation Art
5	Renaissance England	Tanzania & Kenya	Mammals & Primates	Shakespeare
6	Thirty Years' War	Spain	Sound	Baroque Music
7	The Dutch	Netherlands	Light & Optics	Baroque Art I
8	France	Indonesia	Bending Light	Baroque Art II
9	The Enlightenment	Korean Pen.	Color	Art Journaling
10	Russia & Prussia	Central Asia	History of Science	Watercolors
11	Conquistadors	Baltic States	Igneous Rocks	Creative Kids
12	Settlers	Peru & Bolivia	Sedimentary Rocks	Native American Art
13	13 Colonies	Central America	Metamorphic Rocks	Settler Sayings
14	Slave Trade	Brazil	Gems & Minerals	Colonial Art
15	The South Pacific	Australasia	Fossils	Principles of Art
16	The British in India	India	Chemical Reactions	Classical Music
17	Boston Tea Party	Japan	Reversible Reactions	Folk Music
18	Founding Fathers	Iran	Compounds & Solutions	Rococo
19	Declaring Independence	Samoa and Tonga	Oxidation & Reduction	Creative Crafts I
20	The American Revolution	South Africa	Acids & Bases	Creative Crafts II

4	History	Geography	Science	The Arts
1	American Government	USA	Heat & Temperature	Patriotic Music
2	Expanding Nation	Pacific States	Motors & Engines	Tall Tales
3	Industrial Revolution	U.S. Landscapes	Energy	Romantic Art I
4	Revolutions	Mountain West States	Energy Sources	Romantic Art II
5	Africa	U.S. Political Maps	Energy Conversion	Impressionism I
6	The West	Southwest States	Earth Structure	Impressionism II
7	Civil War	National Parks	Plate Tectonics	Post-Impressionism
8	World War I	Plains States	Earthquakes	Expressionism
9	Totalitarianism	U.S. Economics	Volcanoes	Abstract Art
10	Great Depression	Heartland States	Mountain Building	Kinds of Art
11	World War II	Symbols and Landmarks	Chemistry of Air & Water	War Art
12	Modern East Asia	The South States	Food Chemistry	Modern Art
13	India's Independence	People of America	Industry	Pop Art
14	Israel	Appalachian States	Chemistry of Farming	Modern Music
15	Cold War	U.S. Territories	Chemistry of Medicine	Free Verse
16	Vietnam War	Atlantic States	Food Chains	Photography
17	Latin America	New England States	Animal Groups	Latin American Art
18	Civil Rights	Home State Study	Instincts	Theater & Film
19	Technology	Home State Study II	Habitats	Architecture
20	Terrorism	America in Review	Conservation	Creative Kids

Unit 3-5
Printable Pack

This unit includes printables at the end. To make life easier for you we also created digital printable packs for each unit. To retrieve your printable pack for Unit 3-5, please visit

www.layers-of-learning.com/digital-printable-packs/

Put the printable pack in your shopping cart and use this coupon code:

0825UNIT3-5

Your printable pack will be free.

LAYERS OF LEARNING INTRODUCTION

This is part of a series of units in the Layers of Learning homeschool curriculum, including the subjects of history, geography, science, and the arts. Children from 1st through 12th can participate in the same curriculum at the same time - family school style.

The units are intended to be used in order as the basis of a complete curriculum (once you add in a systematic math, reading, and writing program). You begin with Year 1 Unit 1 no matter what ages your children are. Spend about 2 weeks on each unit. You pick and choose the activities within the unit that appeal to you and read the books from the book list that are available to you or find others on the same topic from your library. We highly recommend that you use the timeline in every history section as the backbone. Then flesh out your learning with reading and activities that highlight the topics you think are the most important.

Alternatively, you can use the units as activity ideas to supplement another curriculum in any order you wish. You can still use them with all ages of children at the same time.

When you've finished with Year One, move on to Year Two, Year Three, and Year Four. Then begin again with Year One and work your way through the years again. Now your children will be older, reading more involved books, and writing more in depth. When you have completed the sequence for the second time, you start again on it for the third and final time. If your student began with Layers of Learning in 1st grade and stayed with it all the way through she would go through the four year rotation three times, firmly cementing the information in her mind in ever increasing depth. At each level you should expect increasing amounts of outside reading and writing. High schoolers in particular should be reading extensively, and if possible, participating in discussion groups.

☺ ☻ ☻ These icons will guide you in spotting activities and books that are appropriate for the age of child you are working with. But if you think an activity is too juvenile or too difficult for your kids, adjust accordingly. The icons are not there as rules, just guides.

☺ GRADES 1-4

☻ GRADES 5-8

☻ GRADES 9-12

Within each unit we share:
- EXPLORATIONS, activities relating to the topic;
- EXPERIMENTS, usually associated with science topics;
- EXPEDITIONS, field trips;
- EXPLANATIONS, teacher helps or educational philosophies.

In the sidebars we also include Additional Layers, Famous Folks, Fabulous Facts, On the Web, and other extra related topics that can take you off on tangents, exploring the world and your interests with a bit more freedom. The curriculum will always be there to pull you back on track when you're ready.

You can learn more about how to use this curriculum at www.layers-of-learning.com/layers-of-learning-program/

UNIT FIVE

RENAISSANCE ENGLAND – TANZANIA & KENYA – MAMMALS - SHAKESPEARE

This above all: to thine own self be true.
-Shakespeare (Hamlet Act I, scene III)

	LIBRARY LIST:
HISTORY	Search for: Elizabethan England, Elizabeth I, Sir Walter Raleigh, Sir Francis Drake, English colonies, Spanish Armada, King James I, King Charles I
	☺ ☻ Good Queen Bess: The Story of Elizabeth I of England by Diane Stanley and Peter Vennema.
	☺ Stories From the Faerie Queen by Jeanie Lang. Re-tellings of some of the stories told by Spencer. Free Kindle edition. Read aloud to younger children.
	☺ Elizabeth I: Red Rose of the House of Tudor by Kathryn Lasky. One of the Royal Diaries series. Fictional diary based on factual people and events and conditions. Girls will especially like this one.
	☺ The Redheaded Princess by Ann Rinaldi. Tells the story of young Queen Elizabeth I and her assent to the throne through a perilous youth.
	☺ ☻ Orange and Green by G.A. Henty. About the Irish under the British rule during the reign of Cromwell. The book takes the point of view of the Irish who suffered cruelty under Cromwell's governance of the island.
	☺ ☻ When London Burned by G.A. Henty. Tells the story of the Great Fire of London.
	☺ Life in Elizabethan Days by William Stearns Davis. Tells what life was like for people who lived in Europe during the reign of Queen Elizabeth I.
	☻ Sir Walter Raleigh : Being a True and Vivid Account of the Life and Times of the Explorer, Soldier, Scholar, Poet, and Courtier – The Controversial Hero of the Elizabethan Age by Raleigh Trevelyan. Written by a descendant of Sir Walter Raleigh, the author traveled to all the places Sir Walter himself did and researched this detailed and lengthy book thoroughly. It not only gives a look at one of the most legendary characters in history, but also gives a good idea of England's role in the world and especially on the sea.
	☻ The Faerie Queene by Edmund Spencer. Written during the reign of Elizabeth I and dedicated to her, this is an allegorical epic poem. Save this one for excellent and voracious readers only. The stories told in the poem are entertaining even to a child, but the language is purposefully archaic, obstinately kept that way by modern editors, and is told in poetry rather than prose, always more difficult for the modern reader.

GEOGRAPHY	Search For: Tanzania & Kenya travel guides, Tanzania and Kenya folk tales, Serengeti ☻ ☻ ☻ <u>Wildlife of East Africa</u> by Martin B. Withers and David Hosking. Full of photos of hundreds of animals native to the Serengeti. ☻ <u>We All Went On Safari</u> by Lauri Krebs. A counting picture book takes kids across the plains of Africa where they learn to count African animals in English and Swahili. ☻ <u>Mama Panya's Pancakes</u> by Mary and Rich Chamberlin. A village folk tale from Kenya. ☻ <u>Wangari's Trees of Peace</u> by Jeanette Winter. A true story of a Kenyan woman who went away to school in America and returned to find all the trees cut down. She plants trees in her backyard and then starts a movement to replant all of Kenya. ☻ ☻ <u>Kenya A to Z</u> by Justine and Roy Fontes. Full color photographs take you on a tour around Kenya. ☻ <u>Tanzania</u> by Quintin Winks. From the culture smart series, this book is really written for people planning a trip to Tanzania, but it gives great insight into the culture, customs, manners, and their historical context.
SCIENCE	Search for: mammals, the specific names of particular mammals, primates ☻ <u>About Mammals</u> by Cathryn P. Sill. Part of series, this is a thorough introduction for the youngest kids. ☻ ☻ <u>Crinkleroot's Guide to Animal Tracking</u> by Jim Arnosky. Teaches kids how to identify animal tracks including mammals and birds. Look for other Crinkleroot's Guides. ☻ ☻ <u>What Is A Mammal?</u> by Robert Snedden. Great detail, but simple enough for young kids. ☻ <u>Mammals</u> by Jen Green, David Burnie, and Steve Parker. A DK Eyewitness book.
THE ARTS	Search for: Shakespeare, names of specific plays, Shakespeare sonnets, Shakespeare biography, the Globe Theater ☻ <u>William Shakespeare & the Globe</u> by Aliki. ☻ ☻ <u>Bard of Avon: The Story of William Shakespeare</u> by Diane Stanley and Peter Vennema. ☻ ☻ <u>A Midsummer Night's Dream For Kids</u> by Lois Burdett. A re-telling of the story in easy to understand language, but still with rhyming couplets in the tradition of Shakespeare. Look for other Shakespeare plays in this series. ☻ <u>Shakespeare's Stories For Young Readers</u> by E. Nesbit. ☻ <u>A Young Reader's Shakespeare: A Midsummer Night's Dream</u> by Adam McKeown. A re-telling with beautiful illustrations for the middle grades student. Look for other titles in the series by the same author. ☻ <u>Shakespeare Stories</u> by Andrew Matthews. Look for more by this author. ☻ <u>Tales From Shakespeare</u> by Charles and Mary Lamb. ☻ <u>Tales From Shakespeare</u> by Marcia Williams. ☻ <u>A Midsummer Nights Dream</u> by William Shakespeare, *No Fear Shakespeare* edition. For teens we also recommend <u>Hamlet</u>, <u>Macbeth</u>, <u>Romeo and Juliet</u>, <u>The Taming of the Shrew</u>, and <u>The Tempest</u>. There are many other great Shakespeare plays, so feel free to vary from this list.

HISTORY: RENAISSANCE ENGLAND

Teaching Tip

Kids are all different, so we shouldn't expect the exact same behaviors from all of them. I once visited with a mom who was frustrated because her son was constantly fidgeting and playing with things in the middle of her lessons. I advised her to get him some silly putty and tell him to keep his hands busy while she was talking. He got to fidget, and she got to still feel in control of the lesson and his attention. He was a boy who learned better while DOING, even if the doing had nothing to do with the lesson. Find what works for your kids and you.

Fabulous Fact

James I of England is also James VI of Scotland, so he can be called either in books and often without explanation. He is the monarch who reigned right after Elizabeth I. When she died without heir, James of Scotland inherited the throne of England as well, uniting the two countries in one.

The Renaissance came late to England, almost a hundred years after it was underway in Italy. England was remote and it had been torn apart by the Wars of the Roses. Then, during the reign of Queen Elizabeth I, England was one of the few stable and prosperous realms in Europe. France was embroiled in the wars of religion due to the Reformation. Spain was wealthy from her colonies in the New World, but political uncertainty caused by the Inquisition retarded business and eventually caused Spain to lose many of her colonies and all of her wealth. Eastern Europe, clear through Germany, still groaned under serfdom, was embroiled in wars that would kill off huge percentages of the population, and hadn't really recovered from the depredations of the Ottomans, the Teutonic Knights, and the Mongols before them. Italy had already passed her zenith as a world power and a center of art and culture. The Catholic Church had lost almost all of its political power and much of its wealth during the Reformation movement, and the New World was still in its infancy.

This is Elizabeth I right after the defeat of the Spanish Armada. Her hand rests on a globe to show how her international power is growing.

Equally important, Elizabeth was fiscally responsible during her reign. She had inherited a great deal of debt from her predecessors, but her careful husbanding of the nation's resources cleared the debt and eventually Elizabeth built up a surplus, which left her in position to take advantage of prosperous deals around the globe. Because of the stable political environment and peaceful conditions under Queen Elizabeth, England left her reign ready to climb to the top of the pile in terms of world power. Following hard on the heels of Elizabeth's reign, Britain was establishing colonies in America, in India, in Africa, and the Far East.

Elizabeth, who never married, died without an heir. James VI of Scotland was the next in line to the throne, though his claim was rather distant. He and Elizabeth shared a great grandmother. But James and William Cecil, Elizabeth's secretary of state, had made secret arrangements to secure the succession peacefully, which they managed to do, an incredible feat, as a monarch dying without a clear heir usually led a country into war. So James became king of England as well as king of Scotland, but the two realms were not united under the same parliament and laws until over seventy years later.

James was a mostly good king, who secured peace and prosperity for England and set the stage for the peaceful uniting of England and Scotland. James believed in the divine right of kings and that parliaments were, at best, a necessary evil. He tried to rule without his parliaments as much as he was able. He thought that if God made him king, then as king he could do whatever he liked through royal prerogative. He passed this belief on to his son, Charles I. Charles I pushed his luck, running roughshod over parliament and ruling as an autocrat. His behavior led to a rift in the country, with one faction of parliamentarians who wanted to have a king constrained by parliament and another faction of royalists who wanted to promote the absolute power of the king. Eventually this disagreement erupted into civil war and more than a decade of unrest.

☺ ☻ ☻ **EXPLORATION: Timeline**
- 1558-1603 Queen Elizabeth I reigns
- 1564-1616 Life of William Shakespeare
- 1585-1604 Anglo Spanish War
- 1588 Spanish Armada is defeated by England
- 1603-1625 James I reigns
- 1604-1611 King James Version of the Bible is translated
- 1605 Gunpowder Plot
- 1625-1649 Charles I reigns
- 1640 Long Parliament
- 1642 English Civil War

Additional Layer

A major reason the British ended up controlling colonies flung across the world was that Britain had built up a powerful navy during the reign of Queen Elizabeth. She who controls the seas controls the trade routes, and the trade routes were the source of wealth and power.

Is that still true today? Who controls the seas today? Who controls trade, if anyone? Does wealth still depend on trade?

More Books

Kathryn Hinds wrote a series "Life in Elizabethan England" with titles: *The City, The Countryside*, and *Elizabeth and Her Court*. They are out of print and hard to find, but if you come across a copy, snatch it up. They are gems!

On the Web

This is a 3-minute mini biography of Queen Elizabeth I.

http://youtu.be/cDg9Ao JYxeY

This is a more extensive biography of her from the BBC for older kids:

http://youtu.be/wstzbaI F-Xo

Famous Folks

Kat Ashley was Elizabeth I's governess and later, her close friend and confidant. She is the one person who remained faithful and stable throughout Elizabeth's life. She taught Elizabeth astronomy, geography, mathematics, history, and four different foreign languages. She also taught Elizabeth manners, morals, and how to guard against all the intrigues and plots at court. Without Kat there would have been no Elizabeth.

Writer's Workshop

The defeat of the Spanish Armada was an extremely pivotal event in world history. What would have happened if the Spanish had won and England became a Spanish colony? Write an alternate version of history with the Spanish coming out on top.

- 1649-1659 Commonwealth, when the Puritans ruled
- 1660-1685 Charles II reigns and the monarchy is restored
- 1666 Great Fire of London

☺ ☻ EXPLORATION: Good Queen Bess

Elizabeth I of England ruled after the brief reigns of her older brother, Edward VI, and her older sister, Mary. Elizabeth was exceptionally well educated, with a thorough understanding of history, politics, geography, mathematics, foreign languages, and astronomy. Elizabeth was a Protestant, but unlike her predecessors she didn't push the religion thing too far. She allowed her subjects to quietly pursue their consciences as long as it didn't interfere with the official government line. She also mostly stayed out of foreign wars, while at the same time gaining political power at home and abroad through diplomacy, through her privateers, and especially through commerce. She was brilliant with money, recovering the depleted treasury and building it up, positioning England to take advantage of the emerging trade with the East.

Elizabeth had quite a circle of influential people around her. After you have learned more about Elizabeth and her reign by watching or reading, make puppets of some of these key figures. Start with a wooden spoon, which can be found very inexpensively in any store that sells kitchen implements. Then add curly ribbon or yarn hair, googly eyes, draw on a mouth with markers, and add clothes made from paper or fabric.

Some of the important people in Elizabeth's life include:
- her childhood governess and lifelong friend, Kat Ashley
- her chief minister and spy master, Francis Walsingham
- her secretary of state and politics guru, William Cecil
- her childhood friend and secret love, Robert Dudley
- her arch-nemesis, Phillip II, the Catholic king of Spain
- her cousin, Mary Queen of Scots, who plotted her death in order to take her throne

☺ ☻ EXPLORATION: Spanish Armada

Spain ruled the seas, a good portion of the Americas, and a hefty chunk of Europe, but she really wanted that pesky England. For one thing, England had been tweaking Spain's nose for years with privateers in the Caribbean. England had also sided with the rebellious Protestant Netherlands. To top it off, England was a nation of heretics.

Spain had to act to protect her interests both in Europe and overseas. The key to England has always been the sea since England is an island nation. Fortunately, Spain had the strongest and most well equipped navy Europe had ever seen.

The Spanish Armada sailed to the Netherlands to meet up with more of her army in order to ferry them over to England, but on their way through the channel the Spanish ships were attacked by the little English ships. Four fierce battles were fought between small, maneuverable English ships and powerful Spanish ships. The Spanish anchored that night off the coast of France near Calais, but during the night the English mounted a surprise attack, sending fire ships among the anchored Spanish fleet. The Spanish panicked and their fleet was scattered. The next morning the English ships were still hounding the Spanish, and they fought a battle that lasted all day. The Spanish were utterly defeated by the upstart English, and the Spanish fleet was beset by storms that carried them north around Scotland and Ireland.

About half of all the Spanish ships were destroyed either in battle or by the storms that followed. Any Spanish sailors who managed to crawl ashore in Ireland were put to death by the local peasants. Spain would never recover from the loss of her Armada, and the stage was set for three hundred years of British supremacy on the sea.

Fabulous Fact

In a weird twist of circumstance Phillip II, lifelong foe of Elizabeth I, was also married to Elizabeth's oldest sister, Mary, until Mary's death.

When Elizabeth became queen, Phillip proposed marriage to her. It was all part of the Catholics versus Protestants game being played in Europe at that time.

Additional Layer

Spain wasn't just concerned because most English people became Protestants; they were also very rightly worried about the fate of those who held on to their Catholic beliefs. Catholics in England were systematically persecuted by the English government for centuries.

Today we're so used to the idea of religious freedom that most people just accept that their co-workers, neighbors, friends, and often family members have beliefs different from their own. We are odd that way compared to much of the history of the world.

Do you think freedom to worship (or not) has had overall benefits to society and individuals or the reverse? Why?

Additional Layer

The battle of the Spanish Armada was a major shift in naval tactics. Up to this point, naval battles were fought hand to hand, but the English shot their cannon from a distance and then ran off before the Spanish could close in.

Often, especially today, we think that innovation in warfare involves only technology, but the greatest innovations have actually come through new tactics. The current terrorist tactics represent a new way of fighting that established governments have not adjusted to yet.

Famous Folks

The first Governor of the East India Company was Sir Thomas Smyth. He was also the first Governor of the Virginia Company, Britain's first colony in North America.

To commemorate their victory the English struck a number of medals, souvenirs for the exultant mobs. You can color in one version of these medals in the coloring sheet you'll find at the end of this unit. In the coloring sheet the words "Flavit Jehovah Et Dissipati Sunt 1588" occur. This means "Jehovah blew with his wind and they were scattered" and the date. On the original medal the word "Jehovah" is written in Hebrew characters, but we changed them to Latin characters for the coloring sheet.

The English believed that the defeat of the Spanish Armada was due in major part to the storms that beset the Spanish and that these storms were sent by God to protect England. The Spanish tried to mount two later attacks on England which were also both defeated by storms. Not only was God perceived as protecting England, but also as protecting Protestantism.

☺ ☻ EXPLORATION: East India Company

The British East India Company was very different from modern companies today. For one thing, they had their own army.

They were formed in 1600 and given a royal charter by Queen Elizabeth I. The charter outlined the way the company was to be set up, what it had power to do, and where it was allowed to operate. The government had a small part in the decision making and, of course, gained a great deal of revenue through taxes. Wealthy businessmen and aristocrats, many of whom served in the Parliament, held shares in the company. When the company prospered, so did they; when the company did badly, so did they. Even though the government had little direct control and only an interest via taxes, the parliament passed many laws favorable to this and other British chartered companies because the majority of the members of the parliament held shares in the company.

It was really the British East India Company and other similar chartered companies and colonies that created

The Red Dragon, one of the early ships belonging to the East India Company.

the British Empire. The British army and the British navy each played a role, but mostly it was these companies with their private armies that conquered places like India, South Africa, and Hong Kong.

Originally the British East India Company had been formed to do commerce in the East Indies, but they ended up doing most of their business in India. For the first 157 years the company only had a few small trading outposts in India. In 1757, the company army fought the Battle of Plassey and took direct control of a large portion of India. It was a commercial company which governed India, not the British crown itself. (In 1858 the crown did take direct control, establishing the Raj).

Imagine if Microsoft got a charter to govern Micronesia. Or if McDonald's got a charter to govern Iraq. It seems odd to us today that such a set-up was allowed, but in many ways it was very functional. Of course, in other ways it was very dysfunctional. For example, the Indian people lost their self-governance and were second class citizens in their own country. Furthermore, the British system solidified the caste system already in place in India, reducing the well being of many hundreds of thousands of people for generations.

The Dutch, the Portuguese, and later the French all vied for trade in the Indian Ocean as well. The trade wars were real wars with battles and sinking ships and sword fights. Eventually, it was the British who became dominant and controlled the trade, fueling the wealth of the British Empire.

Read the actual letter sent by Queen Elizabeth granting permission for the East India Company to form: http://www.sdstate.edu/projectsouthasia/loader.cfm? csModule=security/getfile&PageID=857407. At the end of this unit there is a letter sent from an Indian King to King James a few years later. What were the trade agreements when the British first entered India? What did they become later?

☺ ☻ EXPLORATION: Parliament of England
Over the years the English parliament had gained power and influence. It started back in 1512 at Runnymede when King John was forced to sign the Magna Carta. By the time of Charles I the parliament was in open rebellion to the crown. Charles, like his father before him, tried to rule without parliament and believed that it was against the natural order of things for a king to be constrained by any means. Parliament disagreed and cut off Charles' head.

Famous Folks
Sir Walter Raleigh was one of the most well known people of English society. He was a hero, a fop, and a scoundrel.

This little video is a good introduction:
http://youtu.be/PWoC75nSr6g

Additional Layer
In Unit 3-16 we'll learn more about the British in India.

Famous Folks

King James I of England believed in the divine right of kings, which simply meant that the king was chosen by God and, as such, the king was above his subjects, not constrained by the law, and had the power to hand down whatsoever decree he might wish, to which the people must submit or risk hell-fire. James passed his beliefs onto his son Charles who had his head cut off for being such a fool and believing all that nonsense.

Additional Layer

Make a paper model of Westminster Palace and the Big Ben clock tower. Go here: http://cp.c-ij.com/en/contents/3154/03356/index.html for a free printable model.

Parliament ruled without the aid of a king from 1649-1660. After this time the monarchy was reinstated with Charles' son, Charles II, who was a bit more careful than his father had been. Parliament continued to have an everincreasing role in British politics until today when the Monarchy has little real power at all.

Westminster Palace, where the Parliament of Great Britain meets. Photo by David Iliff. License: CC-BY-SA 3.0

A member of parliament (House of Commons) is called an MP for short. There are two houses in the British Parliament: the House of Lords and the House of Commons. Originally there was only a House of Lords, made up of nobles. The members of the House of Lords were appointed to their positions by the Queen at the advice of the Prime Minister. They used to be automatically admitted to Parliament by virtue of their position as a noble.

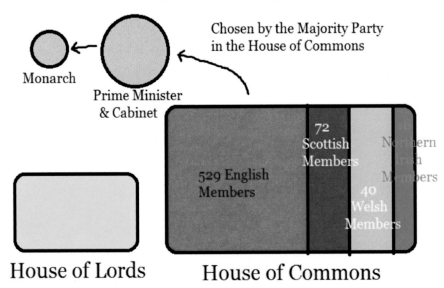

Monarch

Prime Minister & Cabinet

Chosen by the Majority Party in the House of Commons

529 English Members

72 Scottish Members

Northern Irish Members

40 Welsh Members

House of Lords

House of Commons

The members of the House of Commons are elected to represent their districts by a popular vote. There is still a House of Lords and House of Commons today, but nearly all the power rests in the House of Commons, with the Prime Minister and other high government officials being chosen from it. In theory, the Queen is the supreme legislator of the Parliament, but she actually acts on advice of the House of Commons and the Prime Minister.

In 1701, the British Parliament was joined by the Scottish Parliament to create one body. It became known as the Parliament of Great Britain. In 1800, the Irish Parliament was added.

Draw your own diagram of how the Parliament is set up. You can also go online and find out how new laws are made.

☺ ☻ **EXPLORATION: Gunpowder Plot**

In the wee hours of the morning on November 5, the day the first parliament of King James was to meet in their chambers, a man was discovered huddled next to a pile of wood in the cellar of the building. A few feet away were discovered thirty-six barrels of gun powder. The man was Guy Fawkes and he was part of a plot to blow up the parliament, the king and queen, and the king's sons. Guy and his partners were executed for their part in the plot and England breathed a sigh of relief.

The opportunity was not lost on the Earl of Salisbury who used the relief and expansive feeling of the parliament the next day to extract greater sums of money than would have been possible otherwise.

Guy Fawkes became a byword in English society. He also became a really fun holiday. Today in England on the 5th of November people celebrate Guy Fawkes Day, the day the English king was saved, with bonfires and big fireworks displays. Sometimes they also burn effigies, or full sized puppets of straw men dressed in old clothes. They just toss their scarecrows on the bonfire. These days nobody really cares about the origins of the holiday; they 're just in it for a good time.

Schoolchildren in Britain learn this traditional poem to help them remember when the gunpowder plot happened:

On The Web

Make a cool Gunpowder Plot pop-up card using this template:

http://www.activitybuck et.com/creative-crafts/Gunpowder-Plot-pop-up-card

---

Memorization Station

Remember, remember the fifth of November Gunpowder, treason and plot.

I see no reason, why gunpowder treason Should ever be forgot.

Guy Fawkes, guy, t'was his intent To blow up king and parliament Three score barrels were laid below To prove old England's overthrow

By God's mercy he was catch'd With a darkened lantern and burning match.

So, holler boys, holler boys, Let the bells ring. Holler boys, holler boys, God save the king.

And what shall we do with him? Burn him!

Fabulous Fact

Hey, you guys, guess what? In America we say "guy" when we're talking about any male person (and more recently, any person at all). It comes from Guy Fawkes. The British called an oddly dressed person a guy because of the way they dressed the scarecrows they threw on the bonfire. But the bonfire guy had no place in American culture so now we just say "hey, you guys."

Additional Layer

A stylized Guy Fawkes mask has been adopted by anti-government protesters as a way to hide their identity while protesting. It's a take-off from a British comic book series, *V For Vendetta*, which used the Guy Fawkes character as a symbol of rebellion.

The mask has been banned in Canada and Saudi Arabia.

Remember, remember, the 5th of November
The Gunpowder Treason and plot ;
I know of no reason why Gunpowder Treason
Should ever be forgot.

Make a scarecrow Guy Fawkes craft. Glue two craft sticks across the backs of eleven other craft sticks to make the face. Let it dry, then decorate your scarecrow with yarn or raffia hair, a construction paper hat, googly eyes, and markers.

☺ ☺ ☻ **EXPLORATION: Roundheads and Cavaliers**

In 1642 England broke out in war over how the government should function. The two groups fighting were nicknamed the Roundheads and the Cavaliers. The Roundheads were for the parliament and were afraid that the king, who was Scottish, would reduce their English rights. They were also afraid that Charles I, who had married a Catholic French princess would raise his children as Catholics. This could undermine English Protestantism, especially since the king was head of both church and state in England at that time. The Cavaliers believed that the king ought to rule alone, without parliament to interfere, and they wanted to unite Scotland and England into one government, the United Kingdom.

Before the English Civil War the parliament of England only sat in session when the king called for it, which only happened when he needed money. The Parliament controlled the tax revenue and, therefore, the purse strings of the nation.

For eleven years, between 1629 and 1640, Charles managed to avoid calling a parliament. Extremely short on cash, he resurrected old taxes to raise money. This made the English people even more angry. They felt that only parliament should be able to tax them.

To make matters even worse, Charles began to get heavy handed about religion. Laws that had long been ignored were revived and many puritans and non-Anglican members of sects were imprisoned, fined, or had their ears cut off for preaching "sedition." When he moved to implement Anglicanism in Scotland as well, an armed revolt broke out.

He finally made peace with the Scots (they won), but it was expensive. Charles was forced to call parliament to raise funds for the crown. Instead of just giving him money, parliament began to make demands, so Charles shut down the parliament again. The war with Scotland broke out once more. Scotland invaded the north of England; Charles had to respond, but Charles had no money to pay troops or buy weapons and ammunition. He also had to equip his Scottish troops, because he was also the king of Scotland. (Ouch, talk about a sticky spot). He had to call the parliament again.

Parliament's demands were even greater now. They wanted new laws that prevented the king from dissolving the parliament, that allowed the parliament to convene even if he didn't call it, and that made it illegal for the king to raise taxes without the consent of parliament. Charles was forced to concede on every point.

Tensions rose when it was discovered that the Earl of Strafford had offered to raise an Irish army for the king to subdue England. Strafford was beheaded for treason, but distrust for the king rose ever higher. Charles kept blundering, trying again and again to force his will on the English. The parliament kept pushing back. Eventually things became so polarized that nearly everyone in England had picked a side, the king or parliament.

Armed conflict broke out in the fall of 1642. The parliamentary forces won, Charles was captured and imprisoned, dozens of royalist leaders were executed, and an illegal trial of Charles was conducted. The army had taken control of parliament and allowed only those favorable to their cause to conduct the trial. Charles was found guilty of treason and sentenced to death. He was beheaded on January 30, 1649. Later, those who participated in the illegal trial and execution of Charles were imprisoned, exiled, or executed.

On the Web

Videos all about the English Civil War . . .

4 minutes of Horrible Histories fun:

http://youtu.be/3FyQnE Dt7eA

48 minute full on documentary from the BBC about Oliver Cromwell:

http://youtu.be/- TIEURRuGmo

And this 7 minute clip of the trial and execution of Charles I:

http://youtu.be/M3R_Tt VlTmQ

Please preview the last two before showing them to your children.

On the Web

This site has a bunch of interactive maps that show where battles and other important events of the English Civil War happened.

http://www.englishcivil war.org/p/interactive- maps.html

The Battle of Naseby, turning point in the English Civil War

Fabulous Fact

When Charles II was escaping from pursuing armies near Scotland he hid in a tree while soldiers searched for him, one passing directly below at one point. The tree that Charles hid in, is known as the Royal Oak.

Additional Layer

A rough estimate of 866,000 people died or were sold as indentured servants in the New World as a direct result of the English Civil War. Ireland was, by far, the hardest hit with a loss of nearly 41% of its population. The Great Potato Blight Famine only caused a loss of 16% of Ireland's population in comparison.

The Roundheads stepped very firmly on Irish necks and stayed there for the next four hundred years.

After Charles was dead, war broke out once more. The Irish allied with the Royalists to subdue the parliamentary forces in England. But the Roundheads took the fight to Ireland where they prevailed. After the four year war, all Catholic lands were confiscated and given to supporters of the parliamentary cause, all of them English. Ireland has never forgotten.

Charles II, son of the executed king, was declared king of Scotland and he took his throne, raised a Scottish army and invaded England. But it wasn't long before he was fleeing for his life, barely escaping to France. The war was finally over.

Parliamentarians were mostly Puritans who wore their hair short and cropped around their ears and were, therefore, given the derisive nickname "Roundheads." They hated being called Roundheads.

The Royalists were called Cavaliers because it implies a swashbuckling, swaggering gallant, someone dressed extravagantly and not concerned with morals. They wore knee-high leather boots, expensive and fashionably cut tunics, and feathered broad brimmed hats. Their hair was long and dressed in ringlets. They were elitist and royalist to the teeth. Unlike the Roundheads, they embraced the nickname they were given.

At the end of this unit you will find a painting of a Cavalier and a painting of a Roundhead. Print them, cut them apart, and paste them to a poster board. Around each side, Cavalier and Roundhead, write what they stood for, what they wanted, and what happened to them.

☻ EXPLORATION: Oliver Cromwell

Oliver Cromwell became the leading military mind for the Parliamentarians over the course of the Civil War. It was he who personally executed the war in Ireland and Scotland. After the war he ruled as a military dictator for five years. He called himself the Lord Protector.

People are divided over the place in history of Oliver Cromwell. Some see him as a great leader and others as a regicide and genocidal dictator. There is no doubt he was a dynamic and effective leader, able to discipline his troops and meld political factions to his will.

Visit www.olivercromwell.org to learn more about the man, his beliefs, his legacy, and the controversies surrounding him.

This site: www.historylearningsite.co.uk/cromwell_england.htm is a little less kind to Cromwell. After you read about him from these sites and other sources, make up your own mind. Was Cromwell a hero who restored sanity to England and ruled well after a long civil war, or was he a tyrant who let power go to his head? Write your beliefs about Cromwell. Be sure to give specific examples of why you believe the way you do.

☺ ☻ EXPLORATION: The Restoration

England was without a monarch. After Cromwell's death no one could agree on the direction the government should take or who should be in charge. No system was in place to actually govern the nation.

With the prospect of anarchy and further war looming, General George Monck, governor of Scotland, marched troops south into England and called for the return of Charles II from France. Charles agreed to return under certain conditions. Parliament retroactively declared Charles II king from the time his father had been executed, in essence, declaring the intervening attempts at government illegal and void. But it was also well understood that King Charles II ruled with permission of parliament and that they had let him have the throne, and would take it away if his power was abused. The return of the king is called *The Restoration*.

This new relationship between the king and parliament meant that England truly had a constitutional monarchy for the first time.

When Cromwell had been installed as "Lord Protector" he had worn an ermine royal robe, carried a scepter, and sat in the king's coronation chair for the ceremony, but he did not wear the crown or carry the orb. In fact, the Commonwealth government had destroyed the ancestral crown of England which had dated back to Edward the Confessor at least. Cromwell sold the rest of the regalia in order to raise money. When Charles II was reinstated as the monarch of England they needed a new crown. They made what is known today as St.

Famous Folks

After the Great Fire, Sir Christopher Wren's designs for the re-build-ing of London were chosen. He is famous for his design of St. Paul's Cathedral. He also de-signed and built 50 other churches for the city.

On the Web

Gotta love the Horrible Histories, Plague & Fire:

http://youtu.be/943TJb g36T4

And the first 6 minutes of this excellent video uses actual words of people who wrote about the Great Fire:

http://youtu.be/Dn6E_4 g4UAw

On the Web

This site is devoted to the Great Fire of London. It has tons of information and a fun game for kids:

http://www.fireoflondon .org.uk/

Edward's Crown, rumored to be made of the gold of the crown that Cromwell melted down. At the end of this unit you will find a printable of the crown. Color it, cut it out, and add an extra strip of paper to go around your head. On the back of the crown write "Restoration 1660."

☻ ☻ ☻ **EXPLORATION: Plague and Fire**

In the Year 1665 London was hit with a devastating plague made much worse by the overcrowded conditions of the city. Then a year later, in 1666, London was burned to the ground in a massive inferno. Around 100,000 people died in the plague. No one has even a rough estimate of how many died as a result of the fire. At the time, reports were that only a handful had perished, but the poor weren't counted in those days and neither did they count those who died afterward of starvation and exposure.

Plague in 1665.

Read the account by Samuel Pepys, who saw the fire firsthand. http://www.pepys.info/fire.html. With your younger kids, stick to the videos and game on the left hand side of the site.

After you have learned more about the plague and fire, choose one of the events to write a newspaper article about. Select just one point of news and write about the day's events. If you'd like, you can use the picture above as your inspiration for your article.

GEOGRAPHY: TANZANIA & KENYA

Tanzania is on the east coast of Africa bordering the Indian Ocean. Just to the north lies Kenya and just to the south is Mozambique. The ancient land of Zanzibar and Tanganika, located in modern Tanzania, was a center of the Arab slave trade. Arabs would raid cities along the coasts and further inland, capturing and killing as many villagers as possible in their raids. The territory was taken over by Germany and then by the British. In 1961, Tanganyika won its independence. In 1964, Tanganyika and Zanzibar united to become the country of Tanzania.

Fabulous Fact

Most people in both Tanzania and Kenya are Christian.

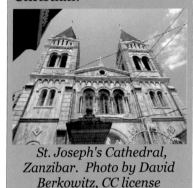

St. Joseph's Cathedral, Zanzibar. Photo by David Berkowitz, CC license

A market in Tanzania. Photo by Fanny Schertzer, CC license

Fabulous Fact

Tanzania is the site of the Great Rift Valley, Mount Kilimanjaro, Serengeti National Park, Gombe National Park, Jane Goodall's chimp research site, Lake Victoria, and Lake Tanganyika. It is the home of wildebeests, gorillas, lions, giraffes, elephants and thousands of other species, including many as yet undiscovered.

After poor experiences with western European governments, the new nation accepted the overtures of the Soviet Union and China and adopted communism. Corruption, forced relocation, and communal farms became the rule. The country was no longer poor; they were now destitute and starving. From the mid 1980's Tanzania has undergone some peaceful political and social reforms, moving away from the communist model and toward more freedom. They are now in recovery and their economy is growing. Tanzania's economy is primarily agricultural, but is rich in natural resources, including gold, precious stones, oil, and gas. Industry is growing and various resources are in the process of being developed. They also have a tourism industry based around their national parks, Serengeti being the most famous.

Famous Folks

President Daniel arap Moi of Kenya was loved by the people of Kenya. He successfully steered the country away from communism, a road their neighbors were taking, and toward more freedom. Finally, in the 1990's, he was able to reintroduce multi-party elections. Toward the end of his tenure more and more stories of corruption and abuse in his administration, including the use of torture, came to light.

Additional Layer

In 2011-2012 Kenya and other east African countries experienced a severe drought. The crops failed and hundreds of thousands of people went hungry, many dying of malnutrition and starvation. International aid stepped in and relieved the immediate hunger, but were criticized, along with local governments, for doing too little too late. What do you think long term solutions to this problem could be?

Kenya is located on the equator with the Indian Ocean on the east and the Great Rift Valley on the west. The climate is mostly hot, except for on Mt. Kenya. As you move from the coast to the northeast the land changes from tropical to arid. The most fertile part of the land is the highlands in the southeastern portion of the nation.

The Germans were the first colonial power in Kenya. The British took control of the country in 1890. More and more white settlers grabbed land for farming coffee and tea in the Kenya highlands, making laws preventing the black natives from owning land or farming coffee. With no way to make a living off the land anymore, the blacks moved en mass to the cities. In the 1950's armed rebellion broke out and was eventually completely squashed by the British. Then, in 1957, the British held open elections and native Kenyans took over the government. They declared and were granted independence in 1963. They set up a constitutional republic, but it was a one party system with institutionalized corruption. This led to several uprisings and attempted coups over the years. In the 1990's the constitution was changed to allow multiple parties, and since the early 2000's the corruption in government took a turn and seems to be improving.

Nairobi, the capital of Kenya.

Kenya is a poor country, but has a wealthier population than any other in east Africa and a small minority of very well off citizens. Advances in educational opportunities for all Kenyans is slowly changing the economic outlook. Their greatest stumbling block is an unstable political environment where chaos breaks out with every election, setting the country back. Education, political stability, and the economy are improving. Tourism is Kenya's biggest economic player right now, followed up by coffee and tea agriculture. Kenya recently discovered oil reserves.

☺ ☻ ☻ EXPLORATION: Tanzania Map

Color and label a map of Tanzania, including cities and natural features. Marking the traditional tribal lands of each of Tanzania's major tribes would be great for an older student to do. You can find a map of Tanzania at the end of this unit.

Label:
- Dar es Salaam
- Zanzibar
- Tanga
- Dodoma
- Mwanza
- Serengeti Plain
- Great Rift Valley
- Masai Steppe
- Great Ruaha River
- Rufiji River

☺ ☻ EXPLORATION: Tanzania Flag

The flag of Tanzania has five oblique stripes in green, yellow, black, and blue. The green represents the land, the gold is for mineral wealth, the black is for the people, and the blue is for the sea. The flags of nations represent their countries in some way, through colors and symbols. Make a Tanzania flag with construction paper, then make your own flag using colors and shapes that represent you or your family. Write or tell about the symbolism of your flag.

☺ ☻ EXPLORATION: Political Discussion

Read more about the political struggles of Tanzania, then discuss how the type of government we live under affects our lives. Communism, democracy, socialism, and republican forms of government have been tried all over the world. Which works best to make the people prosperous and happy?

☺ ☻ ☻ EXPLORATION: Ugali

Try some Tanzanian food, like ugali. Ugali is the main food for most Tanzanians and Kenyans. It's a plain corn porridge to which is added whatever vegetables or meats are available.

> Mix 2 cups corn flour (found as Mexican Masa de Harina in America) and 2 cups water in a bowl. Bring 6 additional cups of water to a boil in a sauce pan. Add 2 Tbsp. butter

Additional Layer

You can find more recipes online to try. Look up Zanzibar Chicken and Chapati Bread.

Additional Layer

If you are eating dinner in Tanzania you had better be dressed comfortably, because you will probably be sitting on a mat on the floor. You will wash your hands both before and after the meal, drying them on a towel that will be passed around from person to person. You will probably drink Squash, the name for any fruit drink in Africa. Almost certainly fresh fruit will be served with your meal. Most, if not all, of the food you are eating was purchased from an open marketplace with lots of fresh foods, live animals, and spices. Ugali will be a staple food at the meal, and you will dip into it with three fingers of your right hand to eat it. Some of your dinner will be a bit spicy. If you are a guest there at dinner, you should end the evening by saying "Asante sana," many thanks for your hospitality.

and a pinch of salt to the water. Stir the corn paste into the boiling water, stirring constantly. Add another 2 cups of flour slowly to the water as you stir. Keep stirring until it has turned into a stiff dough. Serve it with chicken, beef, or any vegetables you like.

Have bananas for dessert; they are cooked in a huge variety of Tanzanian dishes and are important to the diet. Make a fresh fruit pie with bananas, papaya, guava, pineapple, melon and/or oranges in a cooked pie crust. Just cut the fruit up and put it right into the crust. Boil fruit syrup and add a few tablespoons of cornstarch to it to thicken it. Pour the syrup over the fruit and then top it with whipped cream.

☺ ☺ ☻ EXPLORATION: Pests

Tsetse flies are one of the most unpleasant features of Tanzania. They are a biting fly that passes on sleeping sickness. They are such a problem that large areas of Tanzania are unpopulated because of the tsetse fly. They have been completely eradicated on the island of Zanzibar with vigorous programs. Mosquitoes have also caused suffering there by spreading malaria and other diseases.

Research more about the tsetse fly. Draw a picture of the fly and write facts about it around the picture on a large paper or poster board. Present what you've found to a group. Be ready to answer questions.

☺ ☻ EXPLORATION: Serengeti Shadow Box

Make a shadow box of the Serengeti plain. Use a shoebox as the frame. Draw or paint a background of grassy plains and lots of blue sky. In the distance paint in Mount Kilimanjaro. Make paper stand-up animals to place in your box like elephants, wildebeests, lions, gazelles, crocodiles, and hippos. Place a couple of baobab trees in your scenery too. Learn a little bit about each animal and show off and explain your creation.

☺ ☻ EXPLORATION: Make a Toy

Kids in Tanzania don't usually have store bought toys, but they still like to play. Make your own toys out of things you find around the house. Make a doll, a car, or animal figures. Kids all over the world play hide and seek too. Play it the Tanzanian way by shouting "Oh! Oo! Ay!" when you are ready for "it" to come find you. When you're caught, wait by the "monkey tree," a designated home, until everyone is found.

☺ ☺ ☻ EXPLORATION: Run Like An African

Tanzanians have won world-wide acclaim in running events like the Olympics and marathon competitions in major cities. Try running a long distance race like a 5k. Train like an African first by running every single day for four to six weeks before the race.

☺ ☺ ☻ EXPLORATION: Kenya Map

Color and label the map of Kenya you will find at the end of this unit. Label these places with the aid of a student atlas:

- Nairobi
- Mombasa
- Indian Ocean
- Lake Victoria

- Mt. Kulal
- Mt. Kenya
- Tana River
- Galana River

☺ ☻ EXPLORATION: Maasai

Kenya is very tribal, which means that the people divide into factions based on their tribal allegiances and feel little loyalty to their nation or other groups. Each tribe has its own culture, traditions, belief systems, and diet. One of the famous tribes in Kenya are the Maasai, even though they are actually a small minority tribe. The Maasai live in southern Kenya and northern Tanzania. They are also known for resisting changes to their traditional lifestyle. They are nomadic cattle herders and measure their wealth in children and cattle. They wear elaborate and colorful jewelry and brightly colored clothing, red being preferred. Red represents warriors, blood, and bravery, important concepts in the Maasai culture.

Watch this video of some Masaai people doing a welcome dance to western tourists who are visiting their village. http://youtu.be/M2SqPYAh4bM. Increasingly the Maasai are making money from tourism, since their traditional lands are located near the game parks and they have maintained their culture and lifestyle.

Famous Folks

Catherine Ndereba is a world class Kenyan runner. She set the world record time in 2001, won the silver medal in the Olympics twice, and won the Boston Marathon four times.

Additional Layer

The Kibera slum in Nairobi is one of the largest shanty towns in the world, with a population of over 1 million people. Officially it doesn't exist and so receives no government services (water, sewage, garbage service, schools, policing, or health clinics). It is a public health disaster with rampant pollution and crime. Find out more about Kibera, how it started, and what problems it poses. Then think about what could be done to alleviate the problem.

Make your own Maasai beaded necklace craft. Start with a paper plate. Cut it out to leave a large circle to go around the child's neck. Decorate in bright colors using paint, markers, or crayons.

☺ ☻ ☻ EXPLORATION: Kanga Cloth

Women in Kenya and Tanzania often wear Kanga cloth. The cloth is dyed with batik techniques. It has a border along all four sides, a central design, and on one of the long sides also displays a saying, usually in Swahili.

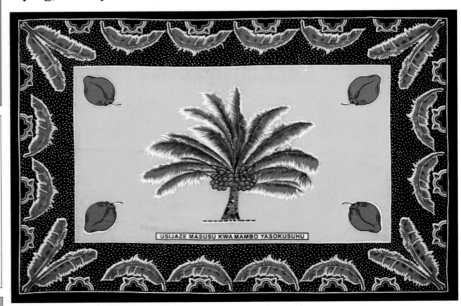

Make your own Kanga cloth.

1. Start with colored gel glue. The gel glue washes out completely and is easy for kids to work with. Make a border along all four sides of a rectangular piece of white muslin cloth, add a center decoration and then write words along the upper edge of one of the long borders. Let the glue dry overnight.
2. Paint in between the lines of your design with watered down acrylic paints. Let it dry overnight again.
3. Soak your cloth in a hot water bath to dissolve the glue. Then dry on a line or in your dryer.

This site: http://www.glcom.com/hassan/kanga.html has many different Swahili sayings found frequently on Kanga cloth.

SCIENCE: MAMMALS

Mammals have hair, give birth to live young, drink milk from their mothers when young, and are warm-blooded. Most mammals have four legs and live on land, but some have two legs or have flippers and fins for life in the water instead of legs. Most mammals are also placental, the placenta feeding the developing baby inside the mother's womb. But there are also marsupial mammals which carry their developing babies and young inside a pouch. In addition, there is a small class of monotremes, which lay eggs. Monotremes include platypus and echidnas.

Kodiak bear, Alaska. Photo by Yathin S Krishnappa, CC license

Mammals have other unique features, including a part of the brain called the neocortex, the outer layers of the cerebral hemispheres. This part of the brain controls sensory perception, spacial reasoning, motor commands, conscious thought, and in humans, language. Lower order mammals have a smooth neocortex. Primates and a few other intelligent mammals have a wrinkled neocortex, lending a much larger surface area. Humans have a very thick neocortex, twice as thick as the next most intelligent mammal, a chimpanzee.

Almost all mammals have seven vertebra in their necks, including giraffes, whales, humans, and bats. Mammals have thick spongy lungs, with very large surface area because of the honeycomb shaped interior. Breathing is driven by a muscle called the diaphragm. The skin of mammals is made of three layers: epidermis, dermis, and hypodermis. The skin also contains sweat glands and hair.

Additional Layer

Marine mammals are another special group of mammals. They have hair, feed their babies milk, are warm blooded, and breathe air, but they live their whole lives in the water and have fins and flippers instead of legs and arms.

Learn more about whales, dolphins, manatees, seals, walruses and other marine mammals.

Writer's Workshop

Choose your favorite mammal and write a "fact and fiction" project. The "fact" is a factual and researched report. The "fiction" is a fun fictional story using your mammal as your main character. Use a two pocket folder and label one pocket "fact" and the other "fiction." Place your writing into each pocket accordingly. Decorate the front cover of your folder with pictures of your mammal.

Additional Layer

Mammals are warm-blooded, which means they maintain their body temperature at a constant even when the surrounding air varies.

Being warm blooded takes a lot of work, so mammals eat more than similarly sized reptiles, birds, or fish. They also have to have ways to keep warm or cool. Mammals have sweat glands and hair. Mammals that live in cold places often have blubber to keep them warm.

Try this experiment to see how blubber works.

http://www.hometrainingtools.com/a/whale-blubber-project

Memorization Station

Memorize the names of the six largest orders of mammals and which types of animals are included in that group.

You can see the orders in the "Classification" exploration to the right. Little ones can learn the common names (rodents, bats, etc.) and older students can learn the scientific names for each group.

☺ ☻ EXPLORATION: Classification

The six largest orders of mammals, by number of species within the order, are Rodentia (rodents, beavers, porcupines), Chiroptera (bats), Soricomorpha (shrews, moles), Primates (monkeys, apes, humans), Cetartiodactyla (even toed hoofed animals, whales), and Carnivora (cats, dogs, weasels, bears, seals).

Make a poster, divided into six sections, and featuring each of the six largest order of animals. Draw or print out species that represent each of these orders and glue them to their section on the poster. You will need to research more about each order to know which animals to include.

☺ ☻ EXPLORATION: Anatomy of a Dog

Use the worksheet at the end of this unit and label the anatomy of a dog. All mammals are similar to one another, though not exactly the same. Your kids should be fairly familiar with this anatomy if they have done the human body. There are only the major internal organs labeled on the dog. Below you see the answers labeled.

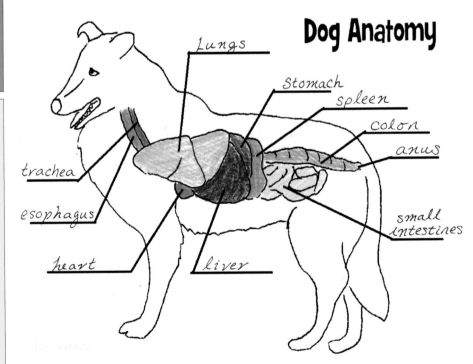

☺ ☻ EXPLORATION: Life Cycle of a Mouse

Color the mouse life cycle worksheet at the end of this unit. If you'd like you can cut apart the sections before the children see it and have them help you reconstruct the order it should be in, coloring and gluing as you go along.

☺ ☺ ☺ EXPLORATION: Build a Bat House

Sometimes while we're outside lying on the ground looking up at the emerging stars on a summer evening the most exciting things we see are the bats catching their evening meal. Bats eat bugs. Lots and lots of bugs. Bats are also the only flying mammal and one of the few creatures that uses echolocation to find their way around.

A bat house is easy to build and it will encourage these flying rodents to live in your neighborhood and eat your bugs. Their natural habitat in the summer is to live in trees, usually in the space between the bark and the trunk , in a hollow tree, or where the bark is peeling away from the trunk. Bats like a tight, narrow space. If you live in a forest you probably don't need a bat house to attract bats, but it can be fun to have one anyway because you'll be much more likely to see the creatures if you already know where to look.

1. Cut plywood according to the dimensions shown below.

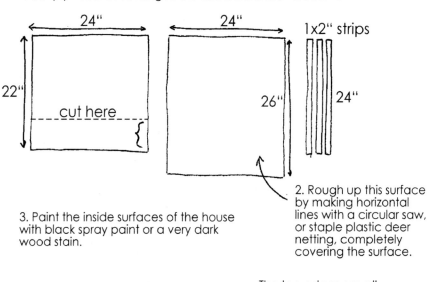

24" 22" cut here

24" 26"

1x2" strips 24"

2. Rough up this surface by making horizontal lines with a circular saw, or staple plastic deer netting, completely covering the surface.

3. Paint the inside surfaces of the house with black spray paint or a very dark wood stain.

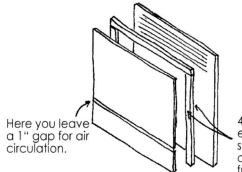

The top edges are all even with one another. At the bottom, the back piece of wood will hang several inches below. This provides a landing plate for the bats.

Here you leave a 1" gap for air circulation.

4. Put a bead of caulk on each side of your wood strips to seal in the heat and keep your wood from gapping.

5. Attach the three layers permanently together with 1" long screws.

6. Paint the outside of the bat house a very dark color if you live in a cool climate and a medium color if you live in a warmer climate.

Fabulous Fact

Echolocation is sonar used by animals to navigate. The animal bounces sound off of objects and when it hears the echo come back, the animal knows how far away the object is and in which direction.

Bats are the most famous animal to use echo-loca-tion, but whales, dolph-ins, and a few kinds of birds do as well.

On the Web

http://www.arkive.org/mammals/

On the Web

If you own a rat, mouse, or guinea pig, you can try this experiment at home:

http://www.sciencebudd ies.org/science-fair-projects/project_ideas/ MamBio_po23.shtml

Another great rodent project is the classic maze. Build a maze from wood, place a piece of cheese or dollop of peanut butter at one end and the rodent at the other. Time how long it takes the rodent to find the treat. Then do it again a second time. Did your animal find its way through the maze more quickly the second time?

On the Web

A short mammal intro:

http://youtu.be/_YSCLS Fm2eA

And here's a 22 min video from the BBC:

http://youtu.be/i4UqjZN 3c0Y

These videos assume evolution. If your views differ, you can take a moment before or after to explain your views to your kids.

Lastly, you need to put a roof on your bat house. The easiest thing to do is to use metal roofing or tar paper and shingles. The roof keeps out the rain and keeps in the heat.

Tips: Hang your bat house in a place that will get lots of sun. About fifteen feet up on the south facing side of a big tree or on the side of an outbuilding or shed would be perfect. Bats like it hot. They'll actually prefer the building if you have an appropriate spot.

Bats also need a nearby source of water. Even a swimming pool or a horse trough or a fake garden pond will do.

☺ ☻ EXPERIMENT: Dissect a Fetal Pig

You can buy a dissection kit for a fetal pig from Home Science Tools or Carolina Biological Supply for about $16. The kit should come with instructions – check that it does.

Use the dissection to learn about the internal organs and structure of mammals.

☺ ☻ EXPERIMENT: Brain Power

The brain is one of the key features that sets mammals apart from other animals. We know that some animals are much more intelligent than other animals. In this experiment we're going to test the intelligence of dogs.

You'll need a large sample size, as many dogs as you can test. Fifty or more would be good. When you test each dog it needs to be in a quiet area by itself for the test to be accurate. You'll conduct three tests on each dog. When you test the dog ask the owner what treat or toy the dog likes; use that object in your tests. It's best if the treat or toy isn't very smelly because we want to test brain power, not nose power. Have the owner there the whole time and have the owner give the dog commands like "sit" or "go."

Keep track of the results in a notebook. Write down the age and breed of each dog along with its scores.

<u>Test 1:</u> Place a treat or toy on the floor in front of the dog, then place a can over the treat or toy. If the dog immediately moves the can to get at the hidden object give it 3 points. If the dog shows interest in the can but is unable to get the treat, give the dog 2 points. If the dog ignores the can give it 1 point.

<u>Test 2:</u> Have the dog sit in front of a table or tray that is just above eye level. Hold a treat above the table where the dog can see it. After the dog makes eye contact, drop the treat or toy onto the table, on a cushion, so it makes no noise. If the dog looks up at the table top give it 3 points. If it looks to the floor then back up the table, give it 2 points. If the dog looks on the floor and never realizes the treat is on the table give it 1 point.

<u>Test 3:</u> Lay two chairs on their sides so that the seats are facing each other and a small gap is left between them. Have a dog sit on one side of the chairs and place a toy or treat on the other side so it is visible between the gap, but the dog can not reach it through the gap. Release the dog. If the dog goes around the chairs and straight to the object give it 3 points. If the dog figures out after some time to walk around the chairs to get the treat give it 2 points. If the dog ignores the treat or tries to go through the gap to get the treat give it 1 point.

Find the mean, median, mode, and standard deviation for each test. Then find the average score on all three tests for each dog.

☺ ☻ ☻ EXPLORATION: Mammal Report

Choose a mammal and become an expert on it. Read books, watch videos, and observe the animal in person if possible. Record the body features, behaviors, eating habits, environment, and life cycle. Think about how the form of the animal's body allows it to do the things it needs to to survive.

When you're done researching, write a report and create a project about your animal. Your project could be a poster board, diorama, a powerpoint, a video, a paper maché reproduction, or any other creative endeavor that interests you.

Additional Layer

In Unit 2-10, when we were studying the human nervous system, we recommended you dissect a sheep brain. If you didn't do it then, you might want to try it now with your high schoolers. Be sure to purchase a dissection guide with your specimen.

This site: http://www.biologycorner.com/anatomy/sheepbrain/sheep_dissection.html

has detailed instructions and photos of the brain dissection.

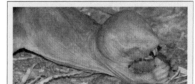

Naked mole rats are a unique mammal because they are cold-blooded, unable to thermoregulate.

On The Web
One of our favorite stops for learning about animals on the web is National Geographic's Creature Feature page. You can look up and learn about all kinds of animals. Have your notepad and pen ready, because you'll learn all sorts of things. They even have some neat video clips along with the reading.

On the Web

The San Diego Zoo has a mammal section on their website. Browse and learn about different species.

http://kids.sandiegozoo.org/animals/mammals

Teaching Tip

You can also print out two sets of the animal cards and play matching games with young kids.

Expedition

Plan several field trips during this unit if possible. You can learn plenty about mammals, but nothing will stick quite like some real time spent with them. Plan to go to a pet store, veteranary clinic, zoo, petting zoo, wildlife refuge, or farm. Arrange to speak with some experts and go prepared with questions. You'll be amazed at how varied and amazing animal life is.

☺ EXPLORATION: Mammal Classification

At the end of this unit you will find printable mammal cards to use for this exploration. Mammals fit into three categories or classifications. They are placentals, marsupials, and monotremes. Placentals carry their young in the womb for a long time until the newborn is fairly well developed. They have a placenta that nourishes the developing animal inside the mother's body. Marsupials give birth to their young when they are still in very early stages of development. The young then finish developing inside the mother's pouch on her abdomen. Monotremes are mammals that lay eggs.

Arrange the animal cards into groups to show which type of mammal each is. If you don't know, you may need to do some research to find out the answers. You will find that many more of the animal cards are placentals than the other two groups. Many more mammals are placentals in nature as well.

☺ ☺ ☺ EXPERIMENT: Respiration Rates

Mammals breathe with lungs which have many compartments, like a honeycomb. This gives mammals a large surface area to take oxygen from the air. But do all mammals breathe at the same rate? You'll need at least two different types of mammals to observe at close range. Household pets and humans will be handy.

Watch your first mammal at rest. Count the number of breaths the mammal takes over one minute. Repeat the experiment at least three times and then take an average of the trials. Now do the same thing with your second mammal. Compare the two. Do they have the same respiration rate?

They are probably different. Think about why they might be different. You can do a little research too. Make a hypothesis and design an experiment to test your hypothesis.

☺ ☺ ☺ EXPERIMENT: Animal Observation

Concentrate on a wild mammal that you will be able to observe with relative ease. Deer, chipmunks, squirrels, mice, bats, or coyotes might be good choices, depending on where you live. Twice a day for a week go to an observation point where you are likely to see the animals. Count how many you see and record what they are doing. See if you can find patterns of behavior. When do they eat? When do they sleep? How large are their family groups or are they solitary animals?

THE ARTS: SHAKESPEARE

William Shakespeare may just be the most recognized name in all of literature. For someone so famous, there's an awful lot we don't know about him. We don't know what he looked like or much about his personal life. We don't know whether or not he went to university. Some even doubt that he actually wrote all of his own plays.

The balcony scene from Romeo and Juliet. Painting by Frank Dicksee, 1884.

He was born in Stratford, England in 1564. His father, William, was a successful local businessman. His mother, Mary, was the daughter of a landowner. In 1582 William, age 18, married an older woman named Anne Hathaway. They soon had their first daughter, Susanna. They had another two children, but their only son, Hamnet, died when he was only 11. After he married, Shakespeare spent most of his time in London writing and performing in his plays. He was away from his family a lot, but his sonnets and plays became the most famous in the world.

Shakespeare died in 1664; we aren't sure how he died, but his vicar suggested it was from heavy drinking. His tombstone is marked with the following epitaph:

Good friend for Jesus sake forbeare
To digg the dust encloased heare
Blessed by y man y spares hes stones
And curst be he y moves my bones

Fabulous Fact

Though there are quite a few portraits made of the bard, we don't actually know what he looked like. They are just artists' best guesses.

Teaching Tip

You can find many or all of Shakespeare's works at most local libraries. They are also available for free on the web.

One other thing – plays were written to be watched, not read. You don't necessarily have to read Shakespeare, especially if you've always thought the bard was boring. Try a video. Your library should have some and you can easily find whole plays online.

But be warned, Shakespeare is bawdy at times. Preview please.

Definitions

Quatrain: a 4-line stanza

Couplet: 2 successive lines that rhyme, they are usually the same length as well.

Famous Folks

Shakespeare wasn't the only famous poet who wrote sonnets. Here are a few others you may recognize:

Elizabeth Barret Browning

William Wordsworth

John Milton

P. B. Shelley

Dante Gabriel Rossetti

Edna St. Vincent Millay

Pablo Neruda

Teaching Tip

Don't be afraid to change the word order to fit the rhythm.

For example, "When **I** look **at** my**self** in **the** mir**ror**" doesn't quite sound right because the emphasis in the word "mirror" is in the first syllable (**mir**ror), not the second. So change it up!

"When **in** the **mir**ror **I** my**self** do **see**."

See? Now you even sound like Shakespeare.

☺ ☻ EXPLORATION: Shakespeare Bulletin Board

Use the coloring sheet of William Shakespeare from the end of this unit to create a poster or bulletin board about him. As you learn more about him throughout this unit, post up the information surrounding his picture.

☺ ☻ EXPLORATION: Shakespeare the Poet

William Shakespeare wrote 154 sonnets, mostly in the 1590's. Fairly short poems, they deal with issues such as lost love. His sonnets showcase his characteristic skill with language and words.

> *"Let me not to the marriage of true minds*
> *Admit impediments. Love is not love*
> *Which alters when it alteration finds,*
> *Or bends with the remover to remove:"*
> -Sonnet CXVI

A sonnet is a poem that expresses a single, complete thought, idea, or sentiment. A sonnet must consist of 14 lines, usually in iambic pentameter (see below), with the rhymes arranged according to a definite scheme. Read several of Shakespeare's sonnets. Memorize your favorite.

☺ ☻ EXPLORATION: Iambic Pentameter

An "iamb" is a variety of the rhythmic unit called a foot. It has a single unstressed syllable followed by a single stressed syllable. Examples of words that naturally follow this pattern include:

to**day**   my**self**   be**cause**   un**less**   to**ward**

Pentameter refers to the need to repeat the iamb five times (penta meaning five). Keep in mind that the iambs don't need to be perfectly built into two-syllable words; they can also stretch out across separate words or even repeat within a single word provided that the stresses still work. Examples include:

- To**day** I **know** I'll **find** my **oth**er **shoe.**
- The **man** I **love** is **quite** a **hand**some **man.**

Try writing some of your own lines in iambic pentameter.

☺ ☻ ☻ EXPLORATION: Rhyme Time

The traditional Shakespearean rhyme scheme is three quatrains followed by a couplet: ABAB CDCD EFEF GG. Each letter stands for the ending sound of the line.

•ABAB means that the first line and the third line rhyme (A with A), as do the second and fourth (B with B).

•CDCD and EFEF follow the same structure as ABAB but with two new word endings; if A and B end in "-oh" and "-ey" sounds, for example, C and D might end in "-us" and "-at," whereas E and F might use "-ing" and "-en" to avoid any overlap.

•GG means that the final two lines of the sonnet rhyme with each other. (That's the couplet.)

Use the Sonnet 18 worksheet from the end of this unit. Write the correct letters by each line to show the rhyme scheme.

☺ ☺ ☺ EXPLORATION: The Globe Theater

The theater where Shakespeare's plays were performed was called The Globe. It was built in 1599 by Lord Chamberlain's Men, the company that Shakespeare wrote for. It closed in 1642 when Cromwell shut down all the play houses. The building was shaped in a circle and was open to the air in the center. Three thousand people could be seated to watch the performances. The poor could watch for a penny from the ground in the center, right in front of the stage. They had no chairs, but stood through the performance. Wealthier playgoers sat in three levels of stadium seats which surrounded the sides and were covered with a roof from above. The stage sat at one side of the circle and protruded into the ground floor area so that people watching nearly surrounded the stage itself. A replica of the theater was rebuilt in the 1990's. You can take a quick tour of it here: http://youtu.be/m3VGa6Fp3zI

Make play posters of some of Shakespeare's plays that could be hung outside the Globe Theater.

Shakespeare's Tragedies

Antony and Cleopatra

Coriolanus

Hamlet

Julius Caesar

King Lear

Macbeth

Othello

Romeo and Juliet

Timon of Athens

Titus Andronicus

Shakespeare's Histories

1, 2, and 3 Henry VI

1 and 2 Henry IV

King John

Henry V

Henry VIII

Richard II

Richard III

On the Web

http://www.classicstage.org/education/schoolprograms/studyguide/

Here are several printable, savable pdf study guides for Shakespeare plays.

These are very, very good. You may choose to do a particular Shakespeare play because these people made an outstanding study guide for it.

On The Web

Curious about the accusations that Shakespeare didn't write his plays? Go visit *The Shakespeare Mystery* at http://www.pbs.org/wgbh/pages/frontline/shakespeare/

You can watch a video on it, explore the discussion boards, and read all about the debate.

On The Web

Spark's Notes has complete copies of many *No Fear Shakespeare* editions online along with study guides.

http://nfs.sparknotes.com/

☺ ☻ EXPLORATION: The Plays of Shakespeare

Select at least one of Shakespeare's plays to do a reading of. Younger children can use condensed versions, like the Lamb's version listed in the library list. We like retellings for younger kids. It helps them to become familiar with great literature so when they are old enough for the adult versions they already know the stories, making it so much simpler.

☺ ☻ EXPLORATION: Hamlet

We're going to walk you through the study of Hamlet and then you can use this same pattern to study other Shakespeare plays.

First watch Hamlet. We like both the Kenneth Branagh version (1996) and the Mel Gibson version (1991). Both plays are best for older kids, with the Gibson version being a bit safer. We recommend the Gibson version if you'll be watching with kids between 11 and 14. Both versions have sexually suggestive scenes plus sword fights and a poisoning scene. If you're concerned, please preview. Be aware that Shakespeare was bawdy and nearly all Shakespeare films will be a bit bawdy as well. You may want to watch more than one version to compare.

Next, read the play. We highly recommend *No Fear Shakespeare* editions which you can purchase in book form or read online at SparkNotes. Here's Hamlet: http://nfs.sparknotes.com/hamlet/

Hamlet's Apparition by Pedro Americo

Read the synopsis and analysis of the play from a study guide like SparkNotes or Cliffs. You may want to watch the play again at this point.

Memorize a passage or soliloquy from the play. You can pick your favorite, but if you're not sure, then we like Hamlet's *what a piece of work is man* speech in Act II, Scene 2. If you'd like, you can do a conversation between two or more characters if you have a partner to memorize with. Besides learning the lines, you should understand what they mean.

Now discuss the play. When doing a discussion begin with simple questions, but not yes and no questions. Then move into the more deep philosophy of what the author is trying to share. We share some discussion points for Hamlet below. Study guides are also helpful.

1. At the beginning of the play the ghost of Hamlet's father appears to the watchmen. What does the ghost represent or foretell? Why do you think Shakespeare uses a ghost in this scene? What atmosphere is set for the rest of the play?
2. The morality of suicide when one is facing unbearable pain is a theme throughout the play. What does Hamlet decide is the right thing to do? What do you believe? There are other moral struggles in the play, especially revenge. How are these resolved?
3. Ophelia is treated like a child by both her father and her brother, Laertes. She is not allowed to make up her own mind about whether she loves Hamlet and how she will respond to him. She never acts, but is only acted upon. Discuss how her inability to act as an adult affects her later fate.
4. How are words used as a tool and weapon in the play? How do characters create a new reality with words? Think about how the old king is killed, with poison poured into his ear. How does this relate to one of the themes of the play?
5. In Act II does Hamlet really go mad, or is he only pretending? Is Polonius a doddering old fool or a clever manipulator? Why are many characters in the play ambiguous?
6. In a play the audience usually knows exactly what is happening and how they should feel about it, while real life is less straightforward. How does the play within Hamlet reflect real life and what are its limitations?
7. The condition of Denmark is tied directly to the condition of its king, "something is rotten in the state of Denmark." Does the moral condition of the state of Denmark get resolved? Which of the characters do you think would make a moral and good ruler? Would Hamlet have been a good ruler if it hadn't been for Claudius?

Finally, chose one of these questions or a discussion point from a study guide and write a paper answering the question in detail. Make sure to include quotes from the play to back up your ideas. The paper should be 1 ½ to 2 pages long, typed, double spaced.

☻ ☻ ☻ **EXPLORATION: Making the Headlines**
Put on a reporter's hat and turn one of Shakespeare's plays into a headline. Write your own newspaper article reporting on the

---

Shakespearean Comedies

All's Well That Ends Well

As You Like It

Cymbeline

The Comedy of Errors

Love's Labour's Lost

Measure for Measure

The Merchant of Venice

The Merry Wives of Windsor

A Midsummer Night's Dream

Much Ado About Nothing

Pericles

The Taming of the Shrew

The Tempest

Troilus and Cressida

The Two Gentlemen of Verona

Twelfth Night

The Winter's Tale

On the Web

We love these coloring sheets of characters from A Midsummer Night's Dream. This is a great play for young kids.
http://www.pheemcfaddell.com/stories/bard/BardPuppetPage.php

Memorization Station

Make your kids memorize (and understand) at least one of these passages. It will change their souls.

http://www.ordo-amoris.com/2011/09/10-passages-from-shakespeare-to.html

This royal throne of kings, Richard II, Act II, Scene I

Tomorrow and tomorrow and tomorrow, Macbeth, Act V, Scene V

Opening soliloquy, Richard III, Act I, Scene I

To bait fish withal, The Merchant of Venice, Act III, Scene I

Shakespeare's Audience

The audience watching Shakespeare's plays represented every class of London life. The cheapest tickets were only a penny, and those were for standing areas only. The higher up you got in the theater, the more expensive the admission prices. The number of people in attendance was quite astounding – about 30,000 weekly theater visitors in a city with a population of about 100,000 people.

events. You can find a newspaper article template on the Layers of Learning website: http://www.layers-of-learning.com/newspaper-article-template/.

For great examples of compelling Shakespeare articles, visit 60 Second Shakespeare at: http://www.bbc.co.uk/drama/shakespeare/60secondshakespeare/themes_index.shtml

☺ ☺ ☺ EXPLORATION: Draw the Scene

After reading (or watching) a scene from one of the plays, draw it. Include background scenes and important characters. Choose a pivotal scene that was important to the play. For younger kids we recommend using one of the excellent retellings (see our library list from the beginning of this unit) instead of the original plays.

The Plays of Shakespeare by Sir John Gilbert. He painted characters from many of Shakespeare's plays all in one scene.

☺ ☺ ☺ EXPLORATION: Act It Out

Act out one or more scenes from a Shakespearean play. You could keep this as simple as a readers' theater or put on a full-blown production with scenery and costumes or puppets. Nothing helps you understand difficult language better than seeing the scene first hand. The kids' versions by Lois Burdett were written to be played. We also recommend these scenes:

Julius Caesar Act III, scenes I and II
Hamlet Act I Scene I

Macbeth Act I, Scene III
The Taming of the Shrew, Act I, Scene II

☺ ☻ EXPLORATION: Make it Relevant
Take the storyline from one of Shakespeare's plays and transform its setting to your town, today. Give the characters current names, current jobs, and current language. Rewrite it for today.

☺ ☺ ☻ EXPLORATION: Famous Last Words
Death was a huge part of Shakespearean plays. There's an easy way to tell a Shakespearean drama from one of his comedies. At the end of a drama, everyone is dead.

Write some of these famous last lines of dying characters on index cards. Take turns imagining the scene that could have gone with the line and acting them out.

Yea, noise? then I'll be brief. O happy dagger!
This is thy sheath;
there rust, and let me die.
　　　　-Juliet, Romeo and Juliet

O, I am slain!
If thou be merciful,
Open the tomb, lay me with Juliet.
　　　　- Paris, Romeo and Juliet

Et tu, Brute! Then fall, Caesar.
　　　　- Julius Caesar, Julius Caesar

No, no, the drink, the drink, - O my dear Hamlet,-
The drink, the drink! I am poison'd.
　　　　- Queen Gertrude, Hamlet

The rest is silence.
　　　　- Hamlet, Hamlet

O true apothecary!
Thy drugs are quick. Thus with a kiss I die.
　　　　-Romeo, Romeo and Juliet

A plague o' both your houses!
They have made worms' meat of me: I have it,
And soundly too: your houses!
　　　　- Mercutio, Romeo and Juliet

And my poor fool is hang'd! No, no, no life!

Additional Layer
The King's Men was the acting company that performed Shakespeare's plays during his lifetime in England. They traveled and performed in theaters as well as for royalty at court. Some years they were unable to perform as scheduled because of the plague's spread through Europe. Shakespeare, himself, was part of the company and acted out many parts in many of his own plays.

Fabulous Fact
Women weren't allowed to act in plays in Elizabethan England, so the female roles were typically played by young men. The theater wasn't really considered a wholesome place for women, so there weren't as many female spectators either.

Writer's Workshop
Writing a play is very different from other writing endeavors because the entire storyline is really driven by dialogue. Your characters must tell the story. Take a story that you've previously written and turn it into a play. You can include stage directions, but it should primarily be dialogue.

Additional Layer

Shakespeare mentions over 600 kinds of birds in his collected written works, including starlings.

Starlings are a European songbird that were imported to America by a fan who wanted to bring all the birds Shakespeare mentioned to the United States. Two flocks of starlings were released in Central Park in New York City. Now there are over a million of them! They have become an invasive species that are driving native species out.

Why should a dog, a horse, a rat, have life,
And thou no breath at all? Thou'lt come no more,
Never, never, never, never, never!
Pray you, undo this button: thank you, sir.
Do you see this? Look on her, look, her lips,
Look there, look there!
     - King Lear, King Lear

☺ ☻ EXPEDITION: Shakespeare Festival

Shakespeare festivals are held all over the country. Look into one in your area. There are also many high schools, universities, and local theaters that perform plays by Shakespeare, and often the admission price is very reasonable. Attend one and watch Shakespeare's work in action.

☺ ☻ EXPLORATION: We Got That One From Shakey

Hundreds of common words and phrases we use today were actually invented by Shakespeare himself. Make and illustrate a booklet of each of these famous sayings from the bard.

"fight fire with fire"
"Knock, knock, Who's there?"
"What's done is done."
"green-eyed monster"
"heart of gold'
"Off with his head!"

"Love is blind."
"Good riddance."
"wild goose chase"
"for goodness' sake"
"so-so"
"in a pickle"

Coming up next . . .
Unit 3-6
Thirty Years War
Spain
Science of Sound
Baroque Music

William Shakespeare

Shakespeare is the most famous playwright in the world. He lived in England during the English Renaissance when many other wordsmiths were living and writing plays. Plays were the entertainment of the day, and Shakespeare's plays were among the best. They are still widely read and performed today.

Renaissance England: Unit 3-5

1558-1603 3-5

Queen Elizabeth I reigns

1564-1616 3-5

Life of William Shakespeare

1585-1604 3-5

Anglo Spanish War

1588 3-5

Spanish Armada is defeated by England

1603-1625 3-5

James I reigns

1604-1611 3-5

King James Version of the Bible is translated

1605 3-5

Gunpowder Plot

1625-1649 3-5

Charles I reigns

1642 3-5

English Civil War

1649-1659 3-5

Commonwealth, when the Puritans ruled

1660-1685 3-5

Charles II reigns and the monarchy is restored

1666 3-5

Great Fire of London

The Great Moghul Jahangir: Letter to James I, King of England, 1617 A.D.

When your Majesty shall open this letter let your royal heart be as fresh as a sweet garden. Let all people make reverence at your gate; let your throne be advanced higher; amongst the greatness of the kings of the prophet Jesus, let your Majesty be the greatest, and all monarchies derive their counsel and wisdom from your breast as from a fountain, that the law of the majesty of Jesus may revive and flourish under your protection.

The letter of love and friendship which you sent and the presents, tokens of your good affections toward me, I have received by the hands of your ambassador, Sir Thomas Roe (who well deserves to be your trusted servant), delivered to me in an acceptable and happy hour; upon which mine eyes were so fixed that I could not easily remove them to any other object, and have accepted them with great joy and delight.

Upon which assurance of your royal love I have given my general command to all the kingdoms and ports of my dominions to receive all the merchants of the English nation as the subjects of my friend; that in what place soever they choose to live, they may have free liberty without any restraint; and at what port soever they shall arrive, that neither Portugal nor any other shall dare to molest their quiet; and in what city soever they shall have residence, I have commanded all my governors and captains to give them freedom answerable to their own desires; to sell, buy, and to transport into their country at their pleasure.

For confirmation of our love and friendship, I desire your Majesty to command your merchants to bring in their ships of all sorts of rarities and rich goods fit for my palace; and that you be pleased to send me your royal letters by every opportunity, that I may rejoice in your health and prosperous affairs; that our friendship may be interchanged and eternal.

Your Majesty is learned and quick-sighted as a prophet, and can conceive so much by few words that I need write no more.

The God of heaven give you and us increase of honor.

English Coin Commemorating the Defeat of the Spanish Armada

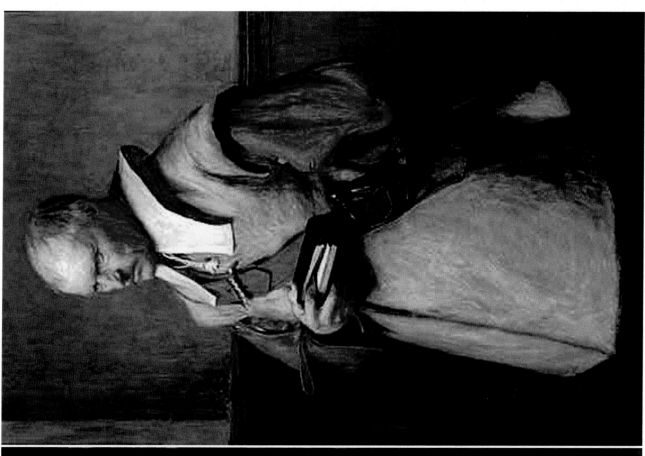

St. Edward's Crown

made for the coronation of Charles II in 1660

Kenya

Tanzania

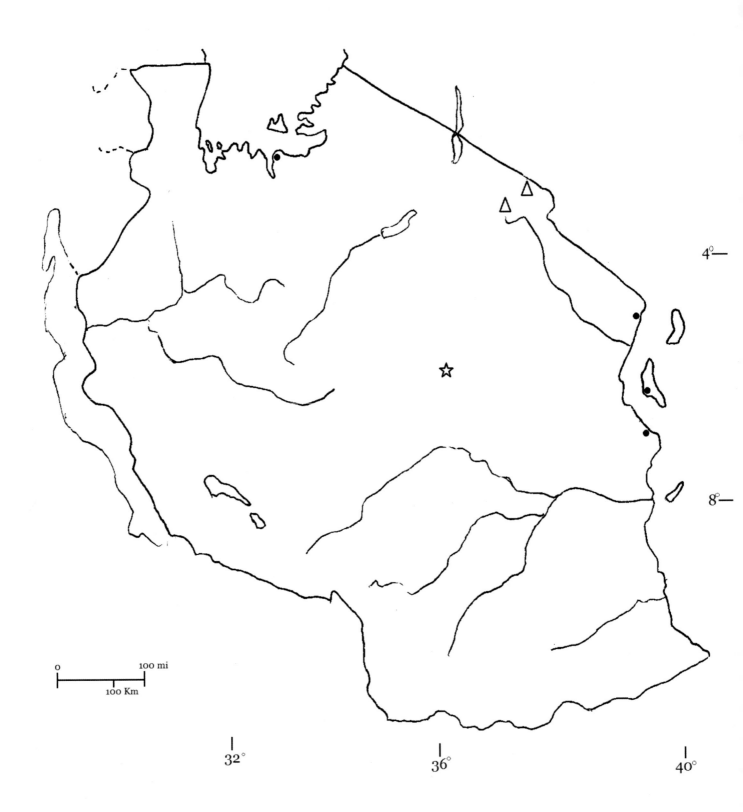

0   100 mi

100 Km

4°—

8°—

32°

36°

40°

Dog Anatomy

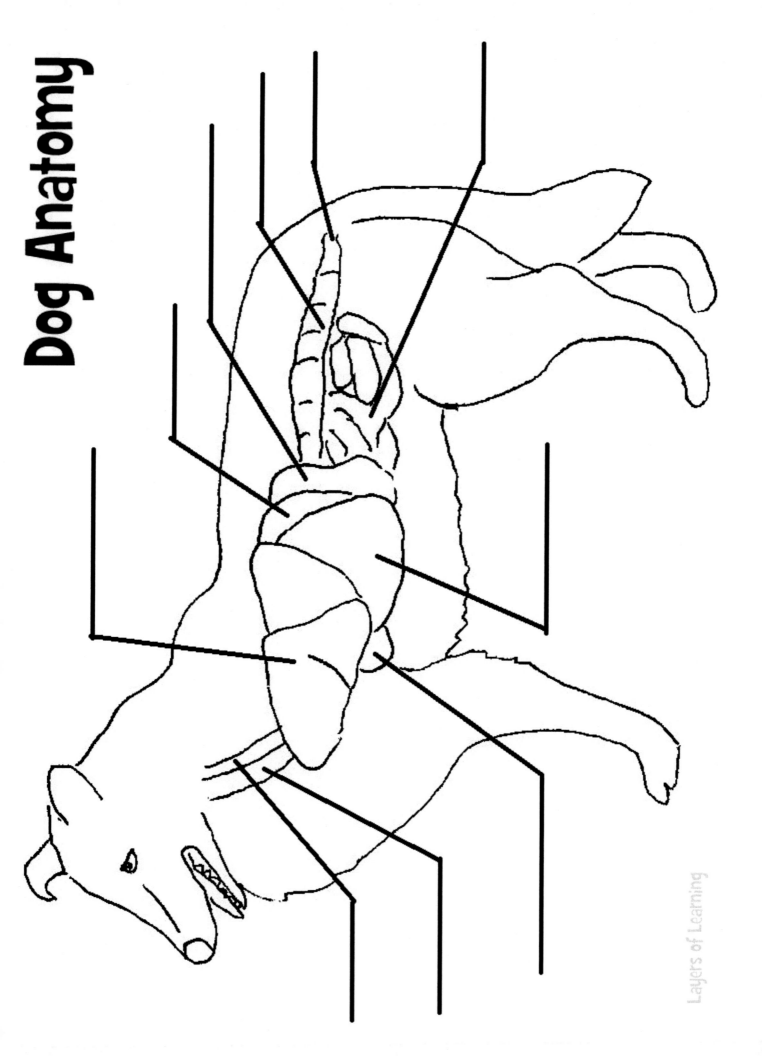

Mouse Life Cycle

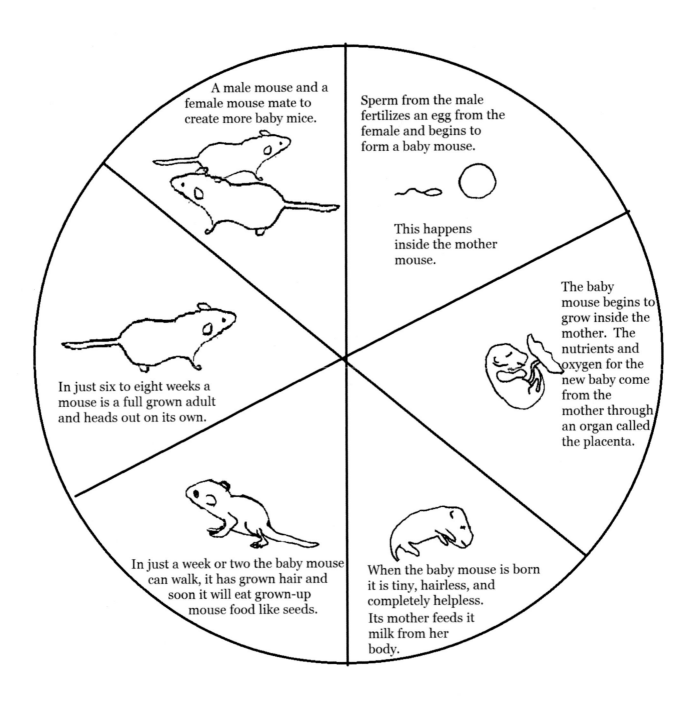

A male mouse and a female mouse mate to create more baby mice.

Sperm from the male fertilizes an egg from the female and begins to form a baby mouse.

This happens inside the mother mouse.

The baby mouse begins to grow inside the mother. The nutrients and oxygen for the new baby come from the mother through an organ called the placenta.

In just six to eight weeks a mouse is a full grown adult and heads out on its own.

In just a week or two the baby mouse can walk, it has grown hair and soon it will eat grown-up mouse food like seeds.

When the baby mouse is born it is tiny, hairless, and completely helpless. Its mother feeds it milk from her body.

cow

fox

dolphin

echidna

kangaroo

wolf

rabbit

human

opossum

platypus

deer

wombat

cat

mouse

zebra

Mammal Cards
Sort the animals into groups of placental, monotreme (egg laying), and marsupial (pouched) mammals.

Sonnet 18

By William Shakespeare

Shall I compare thee to a summer's day?

Thou art more lovely and more temperate:

Rough winds do shake the darling buds of May,

And summer's lease hath all too short a date:

Sometime too hot the eye of heaven shines,

And often is his gold complexion dimm'd;

And every fair from fair sometime declines,

By chance or nature's changing course untrimm'd;

But thy eternal summer shall not fade

Nor lose possession of that fair thou owest;

Nor shall Death brag thou wander'st in his shade,

When in eternal lines to time thou growest:

So long as men can breathe or eyes can see,

So long lives this and this gives life to thee.

ABOUT THE AUTHORS

Karen & Michelle . . .
Mothers, sisters, teachers, women who are passionate
about educating kids.
We are dedicated to lifelong learning.

Karen, a mother of four, who has homeschooled her kids for more than eight years with her husband, Bob, has a bachelor's degree in child development with an emphasis in education. She gardens, teaches piano, and plays an excruciating number of board games with her kids. Karen is our resident Arts expert and English guru {most necessary as Michelle regularly and carelessly mangles the English language and occasionally steps over the bounds of polite society}.

Michelle and her husband, Cameron, have homeschooled their six boys for more than a decade. Michelle earned a bachelor's in biology, making her the resident Science expert, though she is mocked by her friends for being the *Botanist with the Black Thumb of Death*. She also is the go-to for History and Government. She believes in staying up late, hot chocolate, and a no whining policy. We both pitch in on Geography, in case you were wondering, and are on a continual quest for knowledge.

*Visit our constantly updated blog for tons of free ideas,
free printables, and more cool stuff for sale:*
www.Layers-of-Learning.com

Made in the USA
Coppell, TX
27 September 2022

83693902R00033